THE STORY

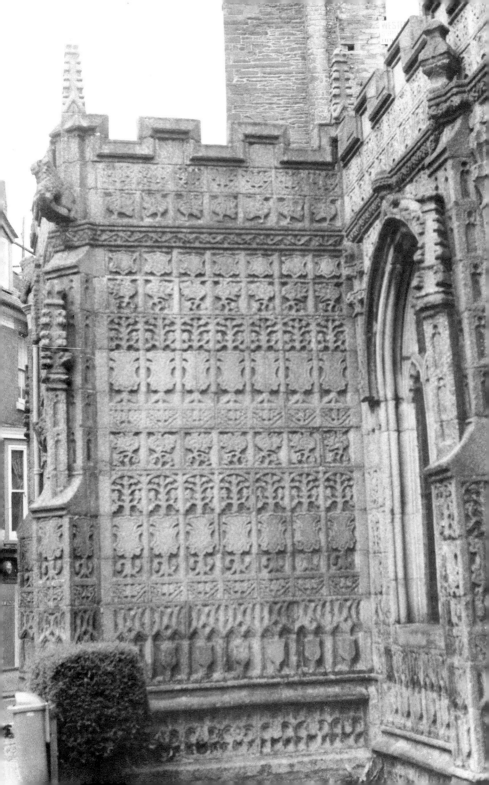

THE STORY OF
CORNWALL'S CHURCHES

S. DANIELL

TOR MARK PRESS . PENRYN

Published by Tor Mark Press, Islington Wharf,
Penryn, Cornwall TR10 8AT.

Second edition 1988
©1988 S. Daniell (text)
©1988 Paul White (photographs)

ISBN 0-85025-300-4
Printed by Swannack Brown & Co., Ltd., Hull, England.

St. Mary Magdalene, Launceston. This notably ornate church was erected in the sixteenth century. The photograph opposite the title page shows the porch, visible on the left of this engraving. All the elaborate panels are carved from extremely hard granite. Great skill and patience, as well as money, must have been employed in this formidable undertaking.

CONTENTS

ORIGINS OF THE CORNISH CHURCH

ONE OF THE MOST INTRIGUING FEATURES of Cornwall's churches is that many are dedicated to saints with the strangest names—St. Buriena, St. Breaca, St. Meriadoc, St. Winwaloe, St. Adwenna, St. Petroc, to name only several of hundreds—names which few people have heard of before. Many of these were Celtic missionaries who came to Cornwall in the fifth and sixth centuries, chiefly from Ireland, but also from Wales and Brittany. Their purpose was to keep burning the flame of Christianity, lit in these islands by the Romans and extinguished, everywhere except in the west, by the subsequent invasions of heathen Anglo-Saxons (English) after 449. Later, in 597, the latter were themselves to be converted to Christianity direct from Rome. In the interim, inspired by the many missionaries, the older Celtic and monastic type of Christianity developed in the remote west of Britain, including Cornwall, on rather different lines.

Each of these missionaries, having chosen the centre for his evangelistic work, set up a shelter, usually of wood. Within lay the sanctuary with its altar, where Mass was celebrated, and outside a Celtic cross of stone was erected. This was the gathering point for those curious or devout enough to watch, and to whom he preached. Soon they too were given protection from the weather and thus there came into being the first churches in the county—nave and chancel, congregation and priest, under the same roof. In following years many of these Celtic oratories must have been built in Cornwall and some of them, made of stone, have survived in part. The sites of many others are indicated by certain of the Celtic crosses, or by old Cornish place names; in many cases, too, there is a church—dedicated to a Celtic saint—now standing on or near the site of his, or sometimes her, oratory.

Opposite: Celtic cross in the churchyard of Lanivet

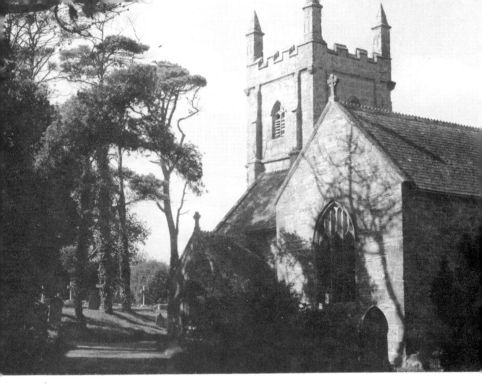

Perranzabuloe. In the twelfth century a new church was erected farther inland to replace St. Piran's oratory, by then overwhelmed with sand. The second building, reconstructed in the fifteenth century, eventually suffered the same fate. In the early nineteenth century most of the fabric was removed to a third site further from the sea, and reconstructed as seen above.

Two of these latter, probably the oldest churches in England, remain in a good state of preservation. Both lie on the Atlantic coast of Cornwall, so close to the sea that at one time or another each has been covered by blown sand and so preserved from the elements and the hand of man. One is at present so buried, a simple rectangular stone building under the dunes at Gwithian, near Hayle. In the nineteenth century it was excavated and found to be 49′ long, 17′ of which comprised the chancel and 32′ the nave. On average it is only about 13′ wide. There is a south door, a stone altar, stone benches within the chancel, and possibly a priest's door and a further window. Less well preserved but probably older than the oratory of St. Gwithian is that of St. Piran, amid the sand dunes north of Perranporth. This little Celtic church, only 25′ by 12′ internally, is of similar layout but with an eleventh century south doorway added later. Overwhelmed by sand from about A.D. 1000–1800 it is today protected from a repetition of this fate by a concrete shell, and is one of two good starting points for anyone interested in Cornish churches or their history.

From the seventh century until the Norman conquest in 1066, there were also churches established in this country by the Anglo-Saxons, but principally in the east. Cornwall, although conquered by them in the eighth century, was little colonised until the tenth, but then only sparsely and, again, in the east. Behind this imbalance of English influence in the county lay the choice in 936 of St. Germans, where a Celtic monastery had existed since the visit of the great missionary St. Germanus of Auxerre in the mid fifth century, as the site of the first cathedral in Cornwall. Regrettably, only a few stones of this important Saxon church remain in that now standing on the same site, but a start in the exploration of Cornish churches may nevertheless logically be made from here. St. Germans and Perranporth could hardly be further apart in Cornwall as points of departure but their positions serve as a reminder of the two differing sources of Christianising influence in Cornwall—Celtic, by sea from Ireland, Brittany and Wales in the fifth and sixth centuries; and Roman, brought first to the heathen Anglo-Saxons of Kent by the Papal missionary, Augustine, in 597.

THE NORMAN CHURCH

A QUARTER OF A MILE east of St. Piran's oratory a Norman church was built about 1150, almost a century after the Conquest. At least until the beginning of the twelfth century few small churches were in fact erected by the invaders, their early years being devoted to the building of castles and to the construction or reconstruction of cathedrals, abbeys and important churches. Thus most of the Norman churches of Cornwall, even the fine one built on the site of the great Saxon church at St. Germans, were relatively late in the period and lacked the extreme simplicity and austerity of eleventh century Norman architecture.

Throughout the country as a whole over 6000 churches, either on entirely new sites or on those of existing buildings, were erected by the religious zeal of the Normans and, despite its remoteness, Cornwall was not entirely neglected in this respect. Some 140 of the present parish churches contain stonework of their Norman predecessors, a large number for a county then so sparsely populated, and attributable in part to the granting of Cornwall to Robert de Mortain, half-brother of the Conqueror.

Most pre-Conquest churches, Saxon or Celtic, were rectangular buildings, comprising sanctuary and nave of approximately the same width, and some of the new Norman structures in Cornwall were to the same design. A large number, however, were cruciform —like a cross laid upon the ground—the sanctuary, with its altar in the east, being the head of the cross, the nave the shaft, and the north and south transepts the arms. In Bodmin church the squat Norman tower, now rebuilt, was placed in a typical position at the head of the north transept, whilst at St. Germans there are twin western towers, the bases of which are of that period. Yet another arrangement is found at Tintagel, where the tower is central. This latter is one of several good examples, relatively unspoilt by additions and alterations, of the Norman cruciform church in Cornwall. It was erected, probably by the Earl of Cornwall, Robert de Mortain, whose castle lay close at hand at Bossiney, as early as about 1100. Nave and chancel are only about 18' wide, and there are two transepts as well as a later little chapel, very likely built over the early Celtic oratory. A west tower was added in the fourteenth century, the original central structure having collapsed. A similar basic plan is found at Crantock, where the tower at the crossing also fell, and was replaced. Other relatively unspoilt examples are St. Enodoc— with a nave $12\frac{1}{2}'$ wide—and Rock chapels, north of the Camel.

The larger and more important churches often had narrow, lean-to aisles added on one or both sides of the nave, and traces of these structures remain in some cases. Morwenstow, for instance, had a

Zennor. A round-headed Norman window, 6" wide and 3' high. It has a wide splay of 3' 3" through the thickness of the wall.

Lelant. Capital and base of a typical Norman pier, showing scalloped decoration.

St. Enedoc. A Norman church, once buried in the sand dunes; it was dug out and restored in 1863. Sir John Betjeman is buried here.

north aisle only, of which the fine arcade remains; St. Issey and St. Breward churches each had a north and south aisle, as did that at St. Germans. The latter is also notable for its Norman clerestory—an upper story of windows—the only example in Cornwall. There are also Norman windows still in existence at Tintagel, Zennor, St. Enodoc and St. Breward. Characteristically they are slit-like—only 4½″ wide at Tintagel—round-headed openings flush with the outside of the wall and opening out into wide splays in its great thickness.

This depth of wall, on average about three feet, was typical of Norman architecture as a whole, and the churches are distinctively heavy and powerful buildings relative to their size—reminiscent in fact of the Norman castle. What might appear to be the natural choice of the Norman mason, Cornish granite, was rarely used, since it was too hard and often too coarsely crystalline to allow of any precision with the axe and pick which were his tools. Instead they quarried softer freestones within the county from Tarton Down, Ventergan and Hicks Grey Mill; they also used the well known Pentewan, Catacleuse and Polyphant stones, serpentine, greenstone, and soft sandstone from the dunes. To these were added imported stone, including the very fine Caen stone from Normandy itself. Those suitable for the purpose were hewn into roughly squared blocks for the main structure leaving, at least in the earlier churches like Tintagel, very wide joints between them. The core of the thick, battered wall was infilled with rubble, squared stone facing it on either side, although a plaster finish was made to suffice on the inner side in some cases.

Dark and cold within, its walls covered with instructive and richly coloured religious paintings, the Norman church in Cornwall was—and still is, if anything remains—to be identified above all by the rounded arch, already encountered in the windows. Typical also are short, cylindrical pillars, plain and massive and, between these and the arches they support, cushion capitals. These are cubical blocks chamfered off in the lower half to fit the round pillar beneath. There are, of course, variations from these but acquaintance with the distinctive nature of Norman architecture, ponderous and powerful, may be made at Morwenstow (north arcade, three west piers and round arches) and St. Germans (south arcade, two west piers—the pointed arches are later). There are examples, too, at Lelant, North Petherwin and St. Buryan. At Morwenstow the capitals, unusually, are circular yet typically each is decorated differently, as are the arches they support; those at St. Germans are

The magnificent Norman doorway of St. Germans

cushion capitals, with a square top or abacus, beneath which is a characteristic pattern of scalloping on the rounded surfaces.

Other guides to this period are the following decorative geometric patterns, and generally speaking, the more profuse the decoration the later the work: the chevron or zig-zag, first to be introduced and very popular by 1150 (Morwenstow arcade, and many doorways, including Landewednack, Cury and the massive portals of Kilkhampton and St. Germans); other motifs followed, including the lozenge i.e. interlocking zig-zag (Cury, doorway); nail-head (doorways of Mylor, Manaccan and St. Stephen-in-Brannel); round pellet (St. Germans capitals); star (Feock, Ladock and Fowey fonts); and bird-beak, i.e. heads with beaks gripping a rounded moulding (Morwenstow arcade, Kilkhampton doorway). Also popular was cable or rope moulding but this was used by the Saxons earlier.

Norman doorway at Manaccan

Landewednack. Norman doorway of serpentine, with typical chevron design. The original door was replaced by a narrower one in the fifteenth century.

Cury. Norman doorway decorated with chevron, lozenge and pellet ornaments. The tympanum is ornamented with interlaced circles.

There are altogether about a dozen fine examples of Norman doorways—usually the most elaborate part of the original church—in Cornwall. They show a wide variety of decorative styles. Five, including Egloskerry and St. Michael Caerhays, also have a simply sculptured tympanum (the area between the round head of the arch and the flat top of the door itself), whilst elsewhere these have subsequently been removed and incorporated into other walls, as at Rame. A number of Norman doorways were transferred to new positions when aisles were added, as at Morwenstow for instance, but when in its original situation the door itself was inset near the centre of the thick wall, with a number of concentric arches and corresponding jambs forming a doorway, a porch almost. Each arch ring was then differently decorated. The classic example in Cornwall is the massive entrance to St. Germans church, with its seven concentric arch-rings and fine chevron mouldings. The south doorways at Kilkhampton and Morwenstow are also outstanding but there are others equally interesting, if more modest, at Cury, Landewednack and Mylor, as well as that at St. Anthony-in-Roseland, which is of Caen stone.

One of the greatest treasures in the Cornish church to survive the passage of centuries is the font. Spared the alterations, additions and restorations affecting the main fabric, and protected from all weathers, it is often the oldest part of the church. There are over eighty Norman fonts in Cornwall, of great interest and often of great beauty. Design, decoration, date and chosen material—granite, sandstone, Polyphant, Pentewan and Catacleuse stones, greenstone and serpentine—vary considerably. Of particular interest, too, are the pre-Conquest fonts at Morwenstow and St. Conan's chapel, Washaway, which are very similar in their extreme crudity of form. Both are roughly circular, without supporting shafts, and are decorated with cable moulding; in the case of the latter there is also the faint 'interrupted interlacing' pattern, so common on the shafts of Celtic crosses but found on no Norman font in Cornwall.

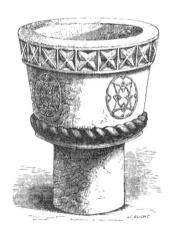

St. Levan. This church in the Land's End peninsula is largely a fifteenth century building but contains an earlier font. This is of the transitional period between Norman and Early English architecture and has both star and cable mouldings.

These two ancient fonts must surely have been of particular religious significance to have been spared by the Normans.

As for the various Norman types, the earliest generally are less crude than the two latter, although also round in shape and simply decorated, as are the single shafts on which they rest. Also circular but of a later date are the sophisticated and beautifully decorated

Lostwithiel. A late Norman font, octagonal in shape. The remarkable relief sculpture depicts a mounted huntsman with hawk and hunting horn. Panels to left and right show the Crucifixion and two lions respectively.

fonts of dark grey Catacleuse stone at Feock, Ladock and Fowey. Over eight centuries old, the mouldings, including the 'star' design, are as sharp as if cut yesterday and probably are from the same hand. Another type is found in north and east Cornwall, at Lawhitton, St. Thomas at Launceston and Altarnun, for instance, characterised by its round, square or octagonal shape with four faces carved at intervals. Later, similar but more elaborately carved fonts were made in which the heads became the capitals of slender decorative sub-shafts, as in the fine examples at Pentewan, Crantock, St. Austell and, above all, Bodmin—a design peculiar to Cornwall.

Manaccan. Early English single and triple lancet windows, the latter grouped together under one containing arch.

BEFORE THE REFORMATION:
ADDITIONS AND ALTERATIONS

DURING THE FOLLOWING three and a half centuries, that is until the Reformation which commenced in 1536, work on Cornish churches was principally devoted to the alteration and expansion of existing buildings in response to an increase both in church ritual and in the county's population. These changes included the lengthening of the chancel to cater for the former, and the enlargement of the old lean-to aisles (or provision of new ones) to cater for both, since aisles could be used for the increasing number of processions as well as for a larger congregation, if need be. Also added were transepts—often used as side chapels; porches, where village business was transacted; and towers for the ever busy church bells, as well as larger windows better to illuminate the dim interior.

These three hundred and fifty years brought with them a gradual evolution of architectural style which may roughly be divided into three periods, together known as Gothic. These are Early English (*c.* 1200–1280), corresponding approximately to the thirteenth century; Decorated, chiefly falling into the first half of the fourteenth century and halted in its development by the Black Death in 1349; and Perpendicular, the late fourteenth, fifteenth and early sixteenth century style which emerged after this major national

Lancet window (left) and Geometric window (right)

upheaval and was brought to an end by another, the Reformation after 1536. Most of the present church architecture in Cornwall belongs to the last period; it is the Early English and Decorated styles which are less frequently encountered.

The Early English style had already made its appearance alongside Norman architecture before the thirteenth century by the introduction of the sharply pointed arch. The windows, which always most clearly typify the architectural style of any of these periods, were long and narrow and larger than their round-headed Norman predecessors, although still splaying out in walls nearly as thick. They are known as lancets (i.e. like a surgeon's knife). At first they occurred singly (St. Allen, chancel; Gerrans nave, north wall), later to be grouped in twos, threes (Manaccan, chancel) or more under one containing arch. Eventually, after about 1250, it became customary to pierce the solid stone in the space above the arched heads of grouped windows to make a smaller light in the shape of a cusped circle, or trefoil (Mylor, tower). In time, this piercing technique was superseded by the Decorated style in which stone mullions were used to form more delicate window-head tracery. At first designs called Geometric and based on the circle were common (quatrefoil, trefoil, etc.), as at St. Ruan Major (south aisle) but gradually increasing elaborate and free-flowing designs patterns called Curvilinear made their appearance. These were extremely varied, and, at their best, of great beauty. On the Continent, this style culminated in Flamboyant (flame-shaped) tracery but in England the Black Death intervened before this development. Examples verging on this type are found at Wendron (chancel); Advent (south aisle—east window); St. Just-in-Penwith (aisles—east windows) and Padstow (south chancel aisle). It was the masons producing these elegant and elaborate windows, and equipped with the delicate chisel instead of the long abandoned Norman axe, whose numbers were soon to be drastically reduced by the arrival of the Black Death in Cornwall.

In the same way during the thirteenth and fourteenth centuries a greater elegance and delicacy of style evolved within the church itself. The pointed arch of the Early English mason was not excessively ornamented with the chevron and other Norman motifs but decorated only with deep-cut multiple mouldings. By degrees, too, the squat, cylindrical Norman pillar gave way to more slender shafts, clustered together to form one pier, while the heavy Norman

Wendron. East window of the chancel, a good example of flowing late Decorated style.

20

Spires at Sheviock (left) and Cubert. The latter is a thirteenth century broach spire, rebuilt in the nineteenth century after being struck by lightning.

capital with its square abacus and geometric ornamentation was super-seded by a round and less cumbersome design and provided with mouldings or carved foliage. Few examples of this period remain in Cornwall; perhaps the best to visit is St. Anthony-in-Roseland with its acutely pointed arches carrying the central tower, foliaged capitals and multi-shafted piers. There is an opportunity to compare Norman and Early English styles side by side at Morwenstow (north arcade—three westernmost arches Norman, two eastern Early English), while the chancel and transept at Manaccan is also of interest. St. Minver (north arcade) and Advent (north transept) are further illustrations. The succeeding fourteenth century Decorated style, continuing the desire to increase the void and diminish the solid, tends towards taller but otherwise similar types of pillars, and wider and flatter arches, as well as more natural foliage as decoration. Simple mouldings continue to be used but are broader and shallower.

A typical motif of this period is the ball-flower (like a globe flower, with opening petals indicated), usually set at intervals within a hollow moulding, as in the south porch at St. Columb Major. This church has one of the few interiors in the county which exemplifies this period; it can also be seen at St. Ive (chancel) and Sheviock (chancel).

During the Early English period of the thirteenth century the building of church towers with spires evolved from the pyramidal roof atop the typical squat Norman tower. Several in Cornwall were used—and perhaps built—as landmarks for mariners, as were towers alone if the church lay near the sea. St. Eval's tower, for instance, was rebuilt at the expense of Bristol merchants in 1727, so well known was its importance to sailors in former centuries. St. Hilary's spire was whitewashed for the same reason, while the dreaded Manacles reef derives its name from 'maen eglos' or the 'church stones', a reference to the spire of St. Keverne upon the skyline near at hand.

An early form of this new architectural feature was the broach spire, in which the latter, octagonal in form, merged into the unparapetted square tower by means of broaches (semi-pyramids) so that the two units were as one. Examples of such thirteenth century towers are Cubert, St. Minver and St. Enodoc. Later, during the Decorated period, the tower was built with the spire rising from the inner, not outer, edges of its thick walls and a parapetted walk for maintenance was thus provided. By the fifteenth century the parapet was battlemented, as at St. Keverne. At this time, however, when most Cornish towers were being built or rebuilt, spires were uncommon.

St. Anthony-in-Meneage. East windows of chancel (left) *and aisle* (right), *both of the Perpendicular period. Note the mullions rising to the head of each window, and the horizontal transoms.*

Bodmin, a fine example of the Perpendicular style

The Black Death, which in 1349 terminated the development of the elaborate Decorated style in England, is estimated to have almost halved the country's population. Church building was for long at a standstill for want of craftsmen, and many were closed for lack of priests. Religious fervour as well as funds for building must also have been lacking long after, but gradually there was a slow recuperation, bringing with it the Perpendicular style of architecture and another great period of church building. Partly because of a shortage of skilled masons, because of a natural reaction to the elaborate style popular before the Plague, and tempered also perhaps by the recent catastrophe, the new architecture was plain. In Cornwall, too, the introduction of granite on a large scale for the first time tended towards even greater severity, for it is normally too intractable for all but the simplest carving; nor did it lend itself to the loftiness and soaring lines which exemplify this style elsewhere. The mediaeval builders must, moreover, always have had in mind the way in which their own cottages, their farm-houses and barns crouched low beneath the sweeping winter gales.

In Cornwall, the surest guide to this style is the window, which best explains the epithet 'Perpendicular'. Flowing tracery is abandoned for slender mullions reaching vertically to or near the much flatter window head; there are also often horizontal stone bars or transoms dividing the whole into panels—briefly, a rectilinear design.

Typically the windows were as large as possible, leaving very little wall between, and this, together with their type of tracery made them ideally suited to the lavish use of painted glass as well as the more recently introduced stained glass, of which sadly so little remains in Cornwall, or indeed elsewhere. Within, the emphasis was also, as far as possible, on the Perpendicular, with slender piers of clustered shafts, simply moulded or foliaged capitals and plainly moulded flat arches. Almost every church contains a great deal of the county's own Perpendicular style of the fifteenth and early sixteenth centuries; Bodmin church, the largest in Cornwall, is a more spacious and lofty example than most, but outstanding also are Kilkhampton, Lanreath, Launceston (exceptional in the intricacy of its granite carving), Launcells, St. Buryan, Golant, Gunwalloe, St. Neot, Probus and St. Austell. In many cases these are in part remarkable because of the beautiful mediaeval church furniture which they contain.

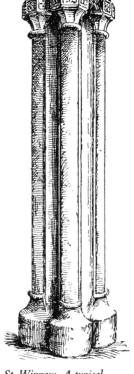

St. Winnow. A typical fifteenth century granite pier of four half-round shafts separated by hollow mouldings. As most Cornish churches were reconstructed during this period, pillars of this kind occur frequently in Cornwall.

The many alterations and additions which embodied these various architectural styles over the centuries produced the typical Cornish church, long and low, and built of granite with a grey slate roof. Both aisles usually run the full length of nave and chancel, often incorporating earlier transepts, and to the outside world exhibiting three parallel pitched roofs terminating generally in a western tower. Most of these latter were erected during the great rebuilding of the Perpendicular period and are usually of granite. Consequently they are neither as lofty or elaborate as their contemporaries elsewhere and in the more exposed parts of the county may be very low indeed. Towednack and Landewednack towers, for instance, are only two stages high, while that of serpentine at St. Ruan Minor has only one stage. Characteristically the Cornish tower is of three

Ruan Minor. The smallest of the little churches of the Lizard, all of which were built to withstand the gales of winter. The tower is of one stage, and only six courses of large serpentine blocks form the walls of the nave.

Towednack. Situated in the windswept Land's End peninsula, the church is a very small building with a simple and massive granite tower of only two stages.

stages, battlemented, with four corner pinnacles roughly carved, and a west door in the lowest stage. Two outstanding examples are Probus' lofty granite tower and that at St. Austell, of Pentewan stone. Both are beautifully ornamented, the former with traceried panels, like a Somerset tower, the latter with eighteen niched figures.

During these centuries prior to the Reformation, the churches of Cornwall acquired many interior features of great interest. Between the chancel, a sacred place set aside purely for the celebration of Mass (preaching took place in the churchyard or at the village cross), and the nave with its congregation a wooden screen was erected during the Perpendicular period. The doors of this were locked to keep the villagers out of the chancel, as well as the dogs which freely followed them into church (there is a dog door for ejecting the latter at Mullion). Above the screen, usually resting on the rood beam, was

Probus. This sixteenth century tower is well known for its height and grace, as well as the traceried panelling which decorates its surface

the Rood itself, a life-sized figure of Christ crucified, with the Virgin Mary and St. John on either hand. The screen comprised wooden posts spaced across the church, each one of which broke into fan vaulting—a Perpendicular innovation—thus making between the posts a row of 'windows'. The heads of these were filled with Perpendicular tracery, but in wood, while beneath were wainscot panels depicting the saints, apostles and the like. The whole, including the rood beam, pillars and fan vaulting, was intricately carved and, together with the Rood, gilded and painted in glowing colours. Behind the Rood was the traditional representation of the Doom while other coloured mural paintings covered most of the walls. Over all arched the typical Cornish wagon or barrel roof of the Perpendicular period, featuring curved braces to the rafters and

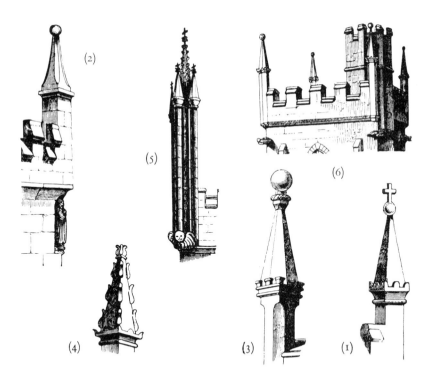

(1) *St. Just-in-Penwith*, (2) *Gulval*, (3) *Sancreed. Typical plain pinnacles carved in tough Cornish granite. The ball or cross is frequently used in ornament.*
(4) *Mullion. Granite pinnacle with simply carved crockets.* (5) *St. Mawgan-in-Meneage. Pinnacles of clustered shafts rise above the graceful tower.* (6) *Buryan. The top of the high tower, which like those at Paul and Gwinear, has a still higher battlemented staircase turret. All three may have been used as watchtowers or for beacons.*

a division of the whole into panels infilled with lath and plaster. These latter were whitewashed to set off the gilded and painted woodwork, beautifully carved and enriched with bosses. Most of these roofs are gone, but a good impression of their former beauty

Buryan. One of the window-like openings or arcades between the pillars and vaults of the rood screen, showing finely carved tracery. Originally each arcade was richly coloured and of different design.

can be gained from visits to St. Endellion, Blisland, Launcells, Lanreath, Madron, Kilkhampton, Morwenstow, Mullion, Poughill and Linkinhorne.

In the same way most rood screens have now vanished, but in some churches—Mawgan-in-Pydar, Gunwalloe, St. Ewe, Lanreath

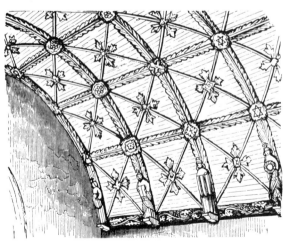

St. Ives. Each carved boss of the wagon roof lies at the intersection of brace and purlin, and the panels formed by these are divided by diagonal mouldings.

and St. Buryan, for instance—sufficient remains for us to visualise the whole. Through them the congregation watched the celebration of Mass at the High Altar and, as seeing in this way was all important, walls which obstructed the view were pierced to make a squint or hagioscope. Examples are found at St. Cury, Landewednack, St. Mawgan-in-Meneage, Quethiock and Landrake. The last two are combined with a stairway to the rood loft, a fifteenth century innovation giving access to the Rood itself.

By the early sixteenth century, most Cornish churches were furnished with oak benches, prior to which there had been few seats available and those watching Mass had been obliged to stand or kneel.

Mullion. Bench ends depicting the Instruments of the Passion. These include the Cross and crown of thorns, the scourge, and the nails, pincers and hammer.

Many of the square-headed carved bench ends fortunately have been preserved, their considerable variety, artistry and liveliness of subject still affording as much pleasure today as they must have done to the mediaeval churchgoers who so often saw them. Notable are those at Mullion, Kilkhampton, Launcells, Mawgan-in-Pydar, St. Winnow, Altarnun and Goran, with others at St. Keverne, Zennor, Landulph, Morwenstow and Poughill. Subjects include a mermaid (Zennor), merman (Gwinear), fiddler, jester, grazing sheep (Altarnun), a ship in a storm (St.Winnow) and a fox preaching to geese (Padstow) but more commonly depicted are the instruments of the Passion, coats of arms or the tools of various trades.

St. Columb Major. A beautiful and dignified fourteenth century building the erection of which was largely financed by the Arundells of Lanherne. This same family also provided for the erection of the fifteenth century tower and its bells. The materials chiefly used were Pentewan stone, and Beer stone from Devon. Notice the three parallel pitched roofs of grey Cornish slate.

THE REFORMATION AND AFTER: DESTRUCTION AND 'IMPROVEMENTS'

WITH THE EARLY SIXTEENTH CENTURY came the religious revolution known as the Reformation. This commenced in 1535 when Henry VIII assumed the position of Supreme Head of the Church of England—although doctrinally still a Roman Catholic—and reached a climax with the excommunication of Elizabeth I in 1570, by which date the Church of England was fully established in this country and Roman Catholicism suppressed.

The retaliatory measures taken against the church in this country during this prolonged quarrel with the Pope were disastrous in Cornwall, as elsewhere. Firstly, the monasteries were suppressed and all their wealth confiscated, bringing about the decline of such

St. Mawgan-in-Pydar. The church is situated in the lovely Vale of Lanherne and is basically thirteenth century with a fine fifteenth century tower. Nearby is Lanherne, the ancient sixteenth century manor house of the Arundell family. Since the eighteenth century this has been a Carmelite convent.

The tower of St. Neot. On the roof is an oak branch, replaced every Oak Apple Day (29 May) in memory, so it is said, of Cornish support for the Royalist cause in the Civil War

great religious centres as Bodmin and St. Germans, whose priories and their churches were destroyed. One might instance also the little priory of St. Anthony-in-Roseland; on its destruction the parishioners claimed the fabric of the church's nave and transepts for their own use (in any church these belonged to and were maintained by the people, who used them for meetings, markets, dancing, drinking and feasting) while the choir of the monks was dismantled by the purchaser of the rest of the priory.

It was then the turn of the parish churches. Firstly, all images, including the precious Rood and any representations of this, were totally destroyed—for instance there is on record the pathetic burning of three pictures of the Rood from Landulph by the Royal Commissioners at Saltash. No sign of any Rood has been found in Cornwall but there is a fine late nineteenth century replacement, with screen and loft, at Blisland. There followed a wholesale destruction and looting of the contents of our churches; stained glass depicting Christ and the saints was shattered, wall paintings obliterated, church plate and jewels confiscated, crucifixes, altars, richly embroidered vestments and altar cloths removed or destroyed. Even the ancient stone altars of the old faith were broken and replaced by wooden tables; of the former several remain wholly or in part, incised as they all were with five crosses representing the five wounds of Christ, including those at Camborne, Towednack and Lanreath. In addition chantry and gild chapels were destroyed. These had come into being in the thirteenth century and the practice was for each to be provided and maintained by an individual or a craft gild; regular Mass was offered within it for the repose of the soul of the donor and his family or in the second case, in honour of the patron saint of the craft. There were for instance three such chapels in the important church of St. Columb Major. Not unnaturally, the interest of lay benefactors as well as the people at large generally declined after such treatment and the fabric of the church, stripped within of almost all that was beautiful and formerly so lovingly maintained to the glory of God, sadly deteriorated. This was particularly so in Cornwall, where the heart had further been taken out of the people's religion by the introduction of the hated English Prayer Book in place of their Latin and Cornish service.

In the seventeenth century yet another orgy of destruction accompanied the Puritan movement. Malicious and fanatical in their striving for even greater simplicity and stricter morality, they swept away anything remaining which might encourage idolatry in the way of statuary, stained glass, crucifixes and altars, rood screens even, while all mural paintings which had survived the Reformation were whitewashed. Their loss seems all the greater to anyone seeing such remnants as there are: at Breage, a mural painting of saints; at St. Keverne and Poughill, of St. Christopher, who safeguarded the worshipper during that day; at Morwenstow, St. Morwenna, the patron saint of the church, on the chancel wall. Then at St. Neot, the mediaeval painted glass depicting the legends of the saint. These windows are perhaps the finest of their kind in England, and it is touching to note that one was subscribed for by the young men of the village, another by the girls. St. Winnow also has most beautiful painted glass, of about 1500, and some remains, too, at St. Kew, Lanlivery and Landulph.

It is small wonder that there was little enthusiasm for church building in Cornwall during these troubled times or in the years which followed. Nor was much added to the existing fabric or to the church furniture. In 1547 it became obligatory for every church to have its pulpit—sermons within the church were little known before the Reformation—and a number of these, rather elaborate, survive, as at St. Winnow and Lanreath (Elizabethan), Fowey, Blisland and St. Kew (Jacobean). In the following century one or two new churches were built in the classical style of the Renaissance, distinctively Protestant churches in their cool sobriety after the richness and glowing colours of their mediaeval predecessors. Redruth church, built in 1768 (except the earlier tower) and Helston, in 1762, fall into this category. The earlier church of King Charles the Martyr, Falmouth (1665) shows a peculiar mixture of the Renaissance and preceding Gothic styles.

The coming of the nineteenth century found the churches in Cornwall in a sorry state through neglect. Indeed, more attention had been paid to the building of Methodist chapels due to the many visits of the Wesley brothers, who had come in an endeavour to restore some heart into the religious life of the Cornish people. Many churches by the end of the century were in a ruinous condition: St. Ruan Major, for example, was unfit for worship, being full of damp rot, birds and bats; the vicar of St. Michael's at Rock needed his umbrella inside the church on wet days. These conditions were 'rectified' during the Victorian period, when a wave of enthusiasm for church restoration swept through the land. In Cornwall, the results were usually disastrous. Oak benches were removed, sawn up and hammered into the shape of pulpits, farm settles, sideboards and the like. Pitch pine pews, mass produced and varnished, were installed. Wagon roofs were torn down, again to be replaced with pitch pine, or were stripped of their colour and plaster panels. The masonry of the inner walls was laid bare and pointed, numerous mural paintings which could have been restored finding their way on to the rubble heap as a barrow-load of damp plaster. There was also much meddling in the name of improvement with the main fabric itself.

Nevertheless, the contributions of the nineteenth century were not entirely to be condemned. A number of churches were restored tastefully and with feeling for the fine workmanship of earlier centuries, such as Lanteglos, Lanreath, Creed, St. Winnow, Blisland, St. Michael Penkevil and Crantock. In the middle years of the century, moreover, many new churches were built to serve the growing needs of the county's mining parishes. These included Carnmenellis, St. Day, Chacewater, Baldhu, Mount Hawke and, in mock Norman style, Tuckingmill.

Above: Charlestown, near S. Austell, built in the mid nineteenth century for the then new community
Below: the porch at Blisland

Above: St. Breward. One of the most exposed and elevated churches in Cornwall, situated on the western edge of Bodmin Moor. It was originally a cruciform Norman building, with lean-to aisles

Below: Gunwalloe, dedicated to St. Winwalloe. This has one of the loveliest situations of all Cornish churches but is in danger of destruction by the encroachng sea. Notable are its rood screen and detached bell tower built into the rocky headland

Right: St. Just in Roseland

TRURO CATHEDRAL

TRURO CATHEDRAL WAS, and is, the pride of the county for several reasons. Immense interest was centred upon its building in the late nineteenth century, as it was the first cathedral to be built in England since St. Paul's, the Renaissance building of Sir Christopher Wren, which arose out of the ashes of the Great Fire of London in 1666. Then again, it was the first cathedral to exist in Cornwall since the removal of the bishopric, 800 years before, from Saxon St. Germans to Crediton and then to Exeter, where the Normans chose to build their cathedral of the south-west.

And when all was finished in 1910, after thirty years' sustained effort, there was also its beauty and grandeur, whether viewed from the rim of heights encircling the city or seen distantly against the sky when coming up the lake-like levels of the rustic Truro River from Falmouth. The architect was J. L. Pearson, whose first unusual inspiration was to build in the style of the French, the cathedral soaring above the narrow streets of the city centre, amongst the rather old, rather crooked little houses that had known Truro in its elegant, early nineteenth century hey-day. Cornwall's links with Brittany—religious, racial and linguistic, economic and commercial —were stronger in past centuries, although the Reformation severed some of the most vital of these. Cornishmen and Bretons in days gone by mingled on either side of the Channel without drawing comment, and the Cathedral is a reminder of those days. Moreover, unexpectedly, Pearson chose to build chiefly in the Early English style which, for all its name, was still under French influence in the West of England.

The revival of the ancient see of Cornwall in 1876 was followed by the installation of the new bishop in Truro parish church, which was made the Cathedral church of the diocese. It was decided that the cathedral should be erected on the site of this church—the sixteenth

Truro. The cathedral from the north. An engraving showing its appearance prior to the building of the western and central towers.

century St. Mary's church at High Cross—all of which was destroyed except the south aisle, which was to be incorporated into the new building and which portion was still to be the parish church of Truro.

Several small books have been written on the architecture of the cathedral and here it is possible only to draw attention to a few outstanding features. The exterior is notable for its many spires and spirelets; two of the former crown the twin western towers flanking the tall, narrow west front, which is very French in feeling; one rises from the central tower, and another from the detached campanile or clock tower at the junction of the south transept and St. Mary's aisle. The last named tower has a roof of Cornish copper weathered to a bright viridian green and in its architectural detail is a deliberate attempt to bring together the more elaborate Perpendicular style of St. Mary's aisle with the severe Early English architecture of the rest of the structure. Also of particular interest is the recently completed chapter house, the very modern lines of which are in perfect accord with the cathedral which overshadows it.

Within, the sharp eye might immediately detect the bend in the nave determined by the street outside. But it is the lofty and elegantly simple proportions of slender piers, arches and grouped lancet windows which first really capture the attention and, on progession round the building, the opening up of vista after long vista through a forest of tall pillars. In fine contrast are the intricately carved reredos and Bishop's throne, as well as the complex of pillars and roof groining in the circular baptistery. From the latter is afforded a long prospect along the ambulatory, a narrow passage between the south aisle of the cathedral choir and the parish church. Along this line the two buildings, so different in style and height, are merged successfully as one.

Closer examination will reveal many other interesting features: stained glass of a peculiar richness appropriate to the period; deliberate inconsistencies and variations in detail of design such as would naturally have arisen among a succession of mediaeval craftsmen working over many decades and without detailed plans; the variety of building and ornamental stones, and perhaps above all, the dedications of the stalls on either side of the choir to the Cornish saints— to St. Buriena and St. Breaca from Ireland, for instance, the Bretons St. Meriadoc and St. Winwaloe, and St. Adwenna and St. Petroc from Wales—with whom the story of the Cornish churches really began.

St. Buryan. Note how the graveyard has risen as the result of centuries of interments.

THE CHURCHYARD: WHAT TO LOOK FOR

MOST VISITORS TO A CORNISH CHURCH walk the length of the churchyard path and enter the building without much thought. Yet observation will show that in most cases it is necessary to step down to enter the church. Not that the site of the latter was ever excavated. The level of the graveyard has risen on account of the hundreds, in some instances thousands, of people buried there.

It is quite likely that the earliest interments were non-Christian. Few people realise that many Cornish churchyards are roughly circular, and it is thought that they may have derived this shape

Left: Truro Cathedral is unusual in England in its situation in the town centre of a maze of old streets. In this respect it is often compared with French cathedrals, especially those in Brittany

from the stone circles or the round tumuli (burial mounds) of pagan times. It would have been logical for the early Christian missionary to ease his task of conversion by setting up his sanctuary on or near a place already of religious significance. Kilkhampton and Mawnan churches actually lie within ancient earthworks approximating to this shape, although these may have been fortifications. St. Dennis certainly is within a circular hill fort, hence its name (Cornish, dinas—fort). In time, the Normans introduced the rectangular one acre graveyard—God's acre—and all the more recent Cornish churchyards are of this shape.

In mediaeval times the busiest and largest part of the churchyard lay to the south of the church. People were buried here rather than to its north where, it was believed, the Devil had his territory in the cold and shadow. The south porch was, moreover, that principally used since the Cornish village usually lay south of the church. It is for these reasons that the north aisle was normally the first to be added, whereupon the north entrance was often blocked up. To the south also stood the important churchyard cross, hundreds of which still remain. Some are of great antiquity, reaching back towards the days of the Celtic missionaries. Their variety of design is enormous but most are basically of the wheel-headed Celtic type. The majority are of granite and therefore not intricately carved. Outstanding examples are at Mylor (the largest, 17′ overall), St. Piran's (tenth century or earlier) and Mawgan-in-Pydar (finely carved Pentewan stone). Many churches of past importance, such as St. Buryan, St. Kew and Madron, had crosses also stationed along the tracks leading to them; in the case of Sancreed, these have now been gathered together in the churchyard.

Also of interest are the many slate sundials, headstones, ledgers and monuments which are so distinctively Cornish. Numbers of these are of the superior Delabole slate but the material is generally available and is little affected by weathering, most of the decoration and lettering being still sharply incised, even after as much as four hundred years. The slate monuments are now almost all within the churches for protection against the elements. They form a fascinating study in themselves, depicting as they do, with doublet, breeches, spade beards, ruffs, wide-brimmed hats, bonnets and curls, lace, brocade and all, churchgoers of the past four centuries—men,

Old Celtic cross at St. Denis. St. Denis is an ancient hill fort (dinas = fort) commanding extensive views over the eerie white landscape of the china clay area

Lanivet. A quiet corner of the churchyard with a tenth century coped gravestone

women and their multitudes of children, who loved, filled and helped maintain the churches of Cornwall as few of us do today. Together with the slate headstones of the humbler folk, and the sundials with their jingles, their monuments form a fascinating collection; some are magnificently executed, others drawn by workmen neither artistic nor literate, with letters missing, words misspelt and anatomy sadly awry. Their inscriptions often are at once instructive, amusing, touching. At St. Wenn, for instance, on the sundial a brief and punning 'Ye know not when'; and in Mylor churchyard, the epitaph of one who indeed did not—

'His foot, it slip and he did fall
Help, help, he cried and that was all'.

St. Breward. Sundial on the porch

INDEX

Launcells   24,28,29
Launceston   *2,5,*17,24
Lawhitton   17
Lelant   10,12
Linkinhorne   28
Lostwithiel   *17*
Madron   28,44
Manaccan   14,*18,*19,21
Mawgan in Pydar   28,29,44
Missionaries   7,14
Morwenstow   10,12,13,15,16,21, 28,29,*33*
Mount Hawke   34
Mullion   25,*27,*28,29
Mylor   14,15,19,44,46
Norman Churches   9-17,19
North Petherwin   12
Oratories   7-10
Padstow   20,29
Paul   27
Pentewan   17
Perpendicular   23-25
Perranzubuloe   8
Poughill   28,29,33
Probus   24,25,*26*
Quethiock   29
Rame   15
Redruth   34
Robert de Mortain   9-10
Rock   10,34
Ruan Minor   25
St Adwenna   7,41
St Allen   19
St Anthony-in-Meneage   22
St Anthony-in-Roseland   15,21,33
St Austell   17,24,25
St Breaca   7,41
St Breward   12,*36,47*
St Buriena   7,41
St Buryan   12,28,*43,*44
St Columb Major   22,*30,*33
St Conan   16
St Cury   29
St Dennis   44,*45*
St Endillion   28
St Enedoc   10,*11,*12,*22*
St Eval   22
St Ewe   28
St Germans   9,12-15,32,39
St Germanus   9
St Hilary   22

St Issey   12
St Ives   28
St Just in Penwith   20,*27*
St Just in Roseland   *37*
St Keverne   22,29,33
St Kew   33,34,44
St Levan   *16*
St Mawgan-in-Meneage   27,29,*31*
St Meriadoc   7,41
St Micheal Caerhays   15
St Michael Penkevil   34
St Minver   21,22
St Morwenna   33
St Neot   24,33
St Petroc   7,41
St Piran   8,9
St Pirans   44
St Ruan Major   22,24
St Stephen in Brannel   14
St Wenn   46
St Winnow   *24,*29,33,34
St Winwaloe   7,41
Sancreed   *27,*44
Sheviock   21,22
Tintagel   10,12
Towednack   25,33
Truro   38-42
Tuckingmill   34
Washaway   16
Wendron   20
Wesley Brothers   34
Zennor   10,12,29